GRANDMA'S PRESERVING SECRETS

GRANDMA'S PRESERVING SECRETS

by Peggy Hutchinson

Edited by Mary Norwak

LONDON
W FOULSHAM & CO LTD
New York   Toronto   Cape Town   Sydney

W Foulsham & Co Ltd
Yeovil Road, Slough, Berks, England

ISBN 0-572-00991-7

© W Foulsham & Co Ltd 1978

Printed in Great Britain by
LOWE AND BRYDONE PRINTERS LIMITED
Thetford, Norfolk

CONTENTS

Introduction		7
Chapter One	Jams and Curds	9
Two	Jellies	25
Three	Marmalades	33
Four	Bottling	41
Five	Pickles	44
Six	Chutneys	53
Seven	Dressings, Sauces and Ketchups	67
Eight	Pastes, Butters and Cheeses	73
Nine	Syrups and Minerals	77
Ten	Farmhouse Specials	81
Eleven	Useful Household Recipes	87
Twelve	Freezing	91
Index		94

INTRODUCTION

A well-stocked store cupboard should be the aim of every housewife, with jars of jam, marmalade and jelly, bottles of fruit, pickles, chutneys and sauces. There can be sauces for special occasions, fruit mincemeat for Christmas, and even home-made beauty treatments. Today's housewife can also use a freezer to take care of raw materials from the garden and market, with the result that far less time need be spent in shopping and far more can be spent in more pleasurable gardening or cooking.

Even a small garden can hold enough fruit and vegetables for eating fresh and for preserving, while there are many fruits to be picked from the hedgerows during family expeditions. Many farms now offer a pick-it-yourself service so that everyone can enjoy gathering food which will provide a full store-cupboard for the winter.

JAMS AND CURDS

Jams and curds can be easily made from fruit and sugar with very simple equipment. A large pan is necessary so that the jam can be boiled rapidly without boiling over, and this is best if made in aluminium. Chipped enamel should never be used and copper can spoil the colour of red fruit. A long-handled wooden spoon should be used for stirring so that hot jam does not splash on the hands.

It is a good idea to collect jam jars throughout the year. Honey jars, coffee jars and preserving jars are also suitable for potting jam, and they should be completely clean before use. When the jam has been put into each jar, it should be covered with a waxed disc which will help to keep the jam well and give it a neat appearance. A transparent cover and a label will complete each jar.

Ingredients

Fruit for jam-making should be fresh, sound and not mushy, and it is best slightly under-ripe as very ripe fruit has a reduced sugar content which will affect the setting and keeping quality of the jam. Some fruits need the addition of acid such as lemon juice or redcurrant juice to extract pectin and improve colour and prevent crystallisation – pectin is the essential ingredient which gives jam its setting quality. Cooking apples, currants, plums and gooseberries are high in pectin content and jam made with them always sets well, so they are often mixed with fruit such as strawberries or cherries which do not set well.

Special preserving sugar may be used for jam, but cube or granulated sugar can be used. Brown sugar does not give a good set although it gives a delicious flavour. Honey and golden syrup are delicious but prevent firm setting and it is advisable only to use ¼ honey or syrup to ¾ sugar if you like the flavour.

Preparing the Jam

Fruit must be cooked slowly to extract pectin, soften skins before adding sugar, and to keep a good colour. Once the sugar has been stirred in and dissolved, it must be boiled rapidly without stirring, which will give a higher yield, better flavour and colour. If the sugar is warmed slightly in the oven or on the side of the stove before adding, it will dissolve more quickly, and speed up the cooking process. Most jams take 5–15 minutes' boiling before setting point is reached. This is most easily tested by dropping a little jam on a cold plate and leaving it to cool. If the jam forms a skin, and wrinkles when pushed with a finger, it is ready.

Take the jam off the heat as soon as it is ready, then stir it well before putting into jars and covering. Store jam in a cool, dark, dry place, and inspect it regularly to see that it remains in good condition.

Curds

Curds are made slightly differently from jams and do not keep so long. They are creamy, fruit-flavoured mixtures of eggs, unsalted butter and sugar, which should be cooked in a double saucepan or in a bowl over hot water. Curds are best made in small quantities and put into small jars. They will only keep 2 months in a cool dry place, but can be stored in the freezer. Curds are particularly delicious for tart fillings and spreads, and they can be used as sauces for ices and puddings.

Annfield Plain Blackcurrant Jam

	Imperial	Metric	American
Blackcurrants	1½ lb	750 g	6 cups
Water	1 pint	500 ml	2½ cups
Sugar	3 lb	1.5 kg	6 cups

Strip the blackcurrants from their stems. Put into a pan with the water and boil for 10 minutes. See that the sugar is warm and stir it into the fruit until dissolved. Boil hard to setting point. Stir well and put into jars. Annfield Plain is a village in Co. Durham which is full of clever thrifty housewives. The next two recipes come from them as well.

Annfield Plain Rhubarb Jam

	Imperial	Metric	American
Rhubarb	2 lb	1 kg	2 lb
Sugar	1½ lb	750 g	3 cups
Dates	8 oz	225 g	1¼ cups
Lemon	1	1	1

Wash the rhubarb and cut it into short lengths. Put into a pan and heat gently until the rhubarb softens. Stir in the warm sugar, chopped dates, grated lemon rind and juice. Bring to the boil and boil hard to setting point. Stir well and put into jars.

Annfield Plain Winter Jam

	Imperial	Metric	American
Apples	6	6	6
Lemons	4	4	4
Bananas	6	6	6
Oranges	4	4	4
Water	8 pints	4.5 litres	20 cups
Sugar			

Peel and core the apples and cut them in pieces. Cut the lemons in thin slices, and discard the pips. Peel and slice the bananas. Peel the oranges and cut the flesh into small pieces. Put all the fruit into the water and simmer for 2 hours. Measure the pulp and for each pint/500 ml/2½ cups pulp, allow 12 oz/350 g/1½ cups sugar. Add the warm sugar to the fruit, stir well and boil hard to setting point. Stir well and put into jars.

Fresh Apricot Jam

	Imperial	Metric	American
Apricots	3 lb	1.5 kg	3 lb
Water	1 pint	500 ml	2½ cups
Butter	1 oz	25 g	2 tbsp
Sugar	4 lb	2 kg	8 cups

Wash the apricots and cut them in half, removing the stones. Put the fruit and water into a pan and boil for 10 minutes. Add the butter and warm sugar and stir well to dissolve. Boil hard to setting point. Stir well and put into jars.

Apple Ginger Jam

	Imperial	Metric	American
Apples	2 lb	1 kg	2 lb
Crystallised ginger	1½ oz	40 g	3 tbsp
Sugar	1½ lb	750 g	3 cups
Water	¾ pint	375 ml	2 cups
Lemon	1	1	1

Peel and core the apples and cut them in quarters. Mince the ginger or chop it very finely. Put layers of apple, sugar and a sprinkle of ginger in a bowl and pour on the water. Leave overnight. Put into a pan and simmer for 30 minutes. Add the grated lemon rind and juice, bring to the boil, and boil for 30 minutes until the fruit and syrup are transparent. Stir well and put into jars.

Blackberry Jam

	Imperial	Metric	American
Blackberries	4 lb	2 kg	4 lb
Butter	1 oz	25 g	2 tbsp
Sugar	4 lb	2 kg	8 cups

Wash the blackberries and put into a pan. Bring slowly to the boil, adding a few spoonfuls of water if little juice runs from the fruit. Add the butter and simmer until the fruit is soft. Stir in the warm sugar and boil hard to setting point. Stir well and put into jars.

Blackberry and Apple Jam

	Imperial	Metric	American
Apples	1 lb	500 g	1 lb
Water	½ pint	500 ml	1¼ cups
Blackberries	1 lb	500 g	1 lb
Sugar	2 lb	1 kg	4 cups

Peel and core the apples and cut them into pieces. Put into a pan with the water and boil to a soft purée. Add the blackberries and bring to the boil. Cook until the berries are just soft. Stir in the warm sugar until dissolved. Boil hard to setting point. Stir well and put into jars.

Blackcurrant and Rhubarb Jam

	Imperial	Metric	American
Blackcurrants	2 lb	1 kg	2 lb
Rhubarb	12 oz	350 g	¾ lb
Water	2 pints	1 litre	5 cups
Butter	1 oz	25 g	2 tbsp
Sugar	4 lb	2 kg	8 cups

Strip the currants from their stems and put into a pan. Cut the rhubarb in small pieces and add to the currants with the water. Boil for 5 minutes. Add the butter and boil for 10 minutes. Stir in the warm sugar to dissolve. Boil hard to setting point. Stir well and put into jars.

Blackcurrant Jam

	Imperial	Metric	American
Blackcurrants	2 lb	1 kg	2 lb
Water	2 pints	1 litre	5 cups
Butter	1 oz	25 g	2 tbsp
Sugar	4 lb	2 kg	8 cups

Strip the currants from their stems and boil in the water for 10 minutes. Add the butter and warm sugar and stir well to dissolve. Boil hard to setting point. Stir well and put into jars.

Bramble Curd

	Imperial	Metric	American
Blackberries	6 oz	175 g	1½ cups
Cooking apples	2 oz	50 g	½ cup
Butter	2 oz	50 g	4 tbsp
Lemon	1	1	1
Sugar	8 oz	225 g	1 cup
Eggs	2	2	2

"Bramble" is a country word for "blackberry". For this recipe the fruit should be large and juicy. The curd is particularly delicious for filling tarts or for a sandwich cake when combined with a layer of whipped cream. Put the blackberries into a pan. Peel and slice the apples and add to the berries. Simmer to a pulp and then put through a sieve. Put this fruit purée into the top of a double saucepan or into a bowl over hot water. Add the butter, finely grated lemon rind and juice and sugar. Heat until the sugar has dissolved. Add the beaten eggs and stir well until thick. Put into jars and store in the refrigerator.

Cherry Plum Jam

	Imperial	Metric	American
Cherry plums	3 lb	1.5 kg	3 lb
Water	1 pint	500 ml	2½ cups
Sugar	3 lb	1.5 kg	6 cups

Cherry plums are sometimes known as "Mirabelles", and they are small round plums not much larger than cherries. Put the plums and water into a pan and simmer until the fruit is soft. Lift out as many stones as possible as they come to the surface. Add warm sugar and stir until the sugar has dissolved. Boil hard to setting point. Stir well and put into jars.

Country Jam

	Imperial	Metric	American
Raspberries	8 oz	225 g	½ lb
Small red gooseberries	8 oz	225 g	½ lb
Redcurrants	8 oz	225 g	½ lb
Rhubarb	8 oz	225 g	½ lb
Sugar	2 lb	1 kg	4 cups

This is a useful jam to make at the end of the soft fruit season when there is a little of each kind of fruit left in the garden. Put the raspberries in a pan. Strip the currants from their strings and add to the pan. Top and tail the gooseberries and cut the rhubarb into small pieces. Put into the pan. Simmer the fruit together until it is all soft and the juices have run out. Stir in the warm sugar until dissolved. Boil hard to setting point. Stir well and put into jars.

Crofton Apricot Jam

	Imperial	Metric	American
Dried apricots	8 oz	225 g	1 cup
Water	2 pints	1 litre	5 cups
Apples	2 lb	1 kg	2 lb
Lemons	2	2	2
Sugar	3 lb	1.5 kg	6 cups
Almonds	1 oz	25 g	¼ cup

Cut the apricots in quarters and soak them in 1½ pints/750 ml/4 cups water for 24 hours. Peel and core the apples and cut them up. Simmer them in the remaining water until soft. Add the apricots and their soaking liquid with the finely grated lemon rinds and juice. Boil for 10 minutes. Add the warm sugar and boil to setting point. Meanwhile, blanch the almonds and cut them into strips. When the jam reaches setting point, stir in the almonds and put into jars.

Date Jam

	Imperial	Metric	American
Dates	1 lb	500 g	2½ cups
Water	½ pint	500 ml	1¼ cups
Sugar	8 oz	225 g	1 cup
Lemon	1	1	1

Cut up the dates and simmer in the water for 30 minutes. Add the warm sugar and the finely grated lemon rind and juice. Stir well until the sugar has dissolved, then boil until thick, stirring well. Put into jars. This jam is particularly good for filling tarts and cakes.

Green Gooseberry Jam

	Imperial	Metric	American
Gooseberries	6 lb	3 kg	6 lb
Water	1½ pints	750 ml	3¾ cups
Butter	1 oz	25 g	2 tbsp
Sugar	6 lb	3 kg	12 cups

Top and tail the gooseberries and simmer in the water until soft. Add the butter and warm sugar and stir until dissolved. Boil hard to setting point and pour into jars. Gooseberry jam keeps green if boiled in a copper pan; sometimes a few young nettles were cooked with the fruit and removed before potting to give the same effect.

Lemon Curd

	Imperial	Metric	American
Butter	3 oz	75 g	6 tbsp
Sugar	8 oz	225 g	1 cup
Lemons	2	2	2
Eggs	2	2	2

Put the butter and sugar into the top of a double saucepan or into a bowl over boiling water. Add the finely grated lemon rind and juice. Heat and stir until the sugar has dissolved. Add the well-beaten eggs and stir well over the heat until it is thick enough to coat the spoon like custard. Put into jars and store in the refrigerator as it will not keep long in a store cupboard. Lemon curd is delicious as a filling for tarts and cakes.

Marrow Jam

	Imperial	Metric	American
Marrow	4 lb	2 kg	4 lb
Sugar	3 lb	1.5 kg	6 cups
Lemons	2	2	2
Crystallised ginger	4 oz	100 g	8 tbsp

Cut the marrow into small dice and put into a bowl with layers of sugar. Leave to stand in a cool place for 24 hours. Put into a preserving pan with the finely grated lemon rind and the juice. Add finely chopped ginger and stir well. Heat gently and stir until the sugar has completely dissolved. Bring to the boil and continue boiling for about 45 minutes until the marrow is clear and tender. Put into jars. This is very good as a tart filling, and sometimes I've added the grated rind and juice of 2 oranges as well, which is very delicious.

Orchard Jam (1)

	Imperial	Metric	American
Apples	1¼ lb	625 g	1¼ lb
Grapes	3 lb	1.5 kg	3 lb
Sugar	3 lb	1.5 kg	6 cups
Juice of lemon	1	1	1

Peel the apples and cut them up. Wash the grapes and remove them from their stalks. Put into a preserving pan and simmer to a pulp. Stir in warm sugar and lemon juice and boil hard until clear and at setting point. Pour into jars. This is a good jam to make from windfall apples and from outdoor or greenhouse grapes which are not good enough for table use – either green or black grapes will do. We used to use it a lot for a large jam tart to serve at teatime.

Orchard Jam (2)

	Imperial	Metric	American
Apples	6 lb	3 kg	6 lb
Water	4 pints	2 litres	10 cups
Sugar	3 lb	1.5 kg	6 cups
Oranges	2	2	2
Seedless raisins	2 lb	1 kg	6 cups
Ground cloves	1 tsp	1 tsp	1 tsp
Ground cinnamon	1 tsp	1 tsp	1 tsp

Peel and core the apples and cut the flesh into dice. Boil the water and sugar and then add the finely grated orange rind and the juice, together with the chopped raisins. Simmer together for 15 minutes. Add the apples and spices and boil for 15 minutes. Put into jars. This is lovely for a tart or cake filling, and another good way of using windfall apples.

Raspberry Jam

	Imperial	Metric	American
Raspberries	4 lb	2 kg	4 lb
Sugar	4 lb	2 kg	8 cups

   Put the sugar in an ovenware dish and place in a low oven. Bring the fruit to the boil in a preserving pan. Take off the heat and stir in the hot sugar until it has dissolved. Put the pan back on the heat, bring to the boil and boil for just 5 minutes. Pour into jars. This jam tastes exactly like fresh fruit and is very easy to make.

Rhubarb and Date Jam

	Imperial	Metric	American
Rhubarb	3 lb	1.5 kg	3 lb
Dates	8 oz	225 g	1¼ cups
Sugar	3 lb	1.5 kg	6 cups
Butter	1 oz	25 g	2 tbsp

   Cut the rhubarb into small pieces and put into a preserving pan with the chopped dates and the butter. Bring to the boil, stirring well. Add the warm sugar and stir over low heat until the sugar has dissolved. Bring to the boil and boil hard to setting point. Stir well and pour into jars.

Rhubarb and Fig Jam

	Imperial	Metric	American
Rhubarb	4 lb	2 kg	4 lb
Dried figs	1 lb	500 g	3 cups
Water	3 tbsp	3 tbsp	3 tbsp
Sugar	4 lb	2 kg	8 cups
Root ginger	1 oz	25 g	2 tbsp

Cut the rhubarb into small pieces and chop the figs finely. Put the rhubarb, figs and water into a preserving pan and bring to the boil. Boil hard for 5 minutes. Break up the ginger with a weight and tie it in a piece of muslin to suspend in the pan. Add the warm sugar and stir over low heat until the sugar has dissolved. Boil hard to setting point. Stir well and put into jars. This is a very old-fashioned jam which many people remember from their childhood.

Rhubarb and Ginger Jam

	Imperial	Metric	American
Rhubarb	3 lb	1.5 kg	3 lb
Sugar	3 lb	1.5 kg	6 cups
Crystallised ginger	4 oz	100 g	8 tbsp

Cut the rhubarb into small pieces. Put into a bowl in layers with the sugar, and leave to stand in a cool place for 24 hours. Add the very finely chopped ginger. Simmer gently and stir well until the sugar has dissolved. Bring to the boil and boil hard to setting point. Put into jars. This makes a very good filling for spongecakes.

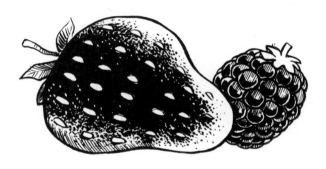

Strawberry Raspberry Jam

	Imperial	Metric	American
Small ripe strawberries	2 lb	1 kg	2 lb
Raspberries	1 lb	500 g	1 lb
Sugar	3 lb	1.5 kg	6 cups

Clean the strawberries and raspberries and put them into a preserving pan. Bring the fruit to the boil and crush it lightly with a wooden spoon so that the juices run. Stir in the warm sugar over low heat until dissolved and then boil hard for 5 minutes. Put into jars.

Strawberry Redcurrant Jam

	Imperial	Metric	American
Redcurrants	2 lb	1 kg	2 lb
Water	½ pint	250 ml	1¼ cups
Small ripe strawberries	2 lb	1 kg	2 lb
Sugar	3 lb	1.5 kg	6 cups

Put the redcurrants and water into a pan and heat gently, mashing the fruit well, so that the juice runs freely. Strain the juice and put into a clean pan with the strawberries. Boil them together for 5 minutes. Add the warm sugar and boil for 5 minutes. Put into jars. The same recipe can be used, substituting raspberries for strawberries.

Strawberry Rhubarb Jam

	Imperial	Metric	American
Small ripe strawberries	2 lb	1 kg	2 lb
Rhubarb	2 lb	1 kg	2 lb
Sugar	4 lb	2 kg	8 cups

Put the strawberries into a preserving pan with the finely cut rhubarb. Bring slowly to the boil and boil for 3 minutes. Add the warm sugar and stir over low heat until dissolved. Bring to the boil and boil for 5 minutes. Stir well and pour into jars.

Chapter Two

JELLIES

Fruit jelly is made by cooking the fruit and water together first and then straining the liquid. This juice is then boiled with sugar to give a bright, clear, firm jelly. Apples, currants and gooseberries make particularly good jelly as they are high in pectin, and they may be mixed with other fruit to give a firm set. When fruit is being used for jelly, skins, cores, and stones may be left while it is cooking, as this will add to the setting quality, and the juice is strained off to leave all debris.

The same equipment is needed as for jam-making with the addition of a flannel jelly bag which must be suspended on a stand, or between the legs of a chair so that the juice drips into a bowl. If a jelly bag is not available, a well-boiled tea-towel can be used instead. When the juice and sugar are boiled together, a little nut of butter should be added, which will prevent scum forming, and will also give brightness to the finished jelly. Test on a plate in the same way as jam, and put jelly into small jars as it is rather special.

Blackcurrant Jelly

	Imperial	Metric	American
Blackcurrants	3 lb	1.5 kg	3 lb
Water	1 pint	500 ml	2½ cups
Sugar			

Wash the currants and simmer in the water for 30 minutes. Put into a jelly bag and leave the juice to drip through. Measure the juice and allow 1 lb/500 g/2 cups sugar to each pint/500 ml/2½ cups juice. Warm the sugar. Bring the juice to the boil, add the warm sugar and boil hard to setting point. Pour into jars.

Bramble (Blackberry) Jelly

	Imperial	Metric	American
Blackberries	4 lb	2 kg	4 lb
Juice of lemons	2	2	2
Water	½ pint	250 ml	1¼ cups
Sugar			

Use slightly under-ripe berries and put them into a pan with the lemon juice and water. Simmer for 30 minutes until the fruit is very soft. Strain through a jelly bag and measure the juice. Allow 1 lb/500 g/2 cups sugar to each pint/500 ml/2½ cups juice. Warm the sugar. Bring the juice to the boil, add the warm sugar and boil hard to setting point. Pour into jars. A pinch of ground nutmeg or cinnamon gives a specially good flavour to this jelly, which is a very old country favourite.

Crabapple Jelly

	Imperial	Metric	American
Crabapples	4 lb	2 kg	4 lb
Water	4 pints	2 litres	10 cups
Sugar			

Wash the fruit and cut it up without peeling or removing cores. Add the water and boil until the apples are soft. Strain through a jelly bag and measure the juice. Allow 1 lb/500 g/2 cups sugar to each pint/500 ml/2½ cups juice. Warm the sugar. Bring the juice to the boil and stir in the sugar. Boil hard to setting point and pour into jars. It is important that crabapple jelly is boiled quickly to setting point so that it keeps a bright red colour – if it is overboiled, it becomes terra-cotta colour. The ornamental Siberian crabapples make a brilliant red jelly with a fine flavour.

Damson and Apple Jelly

	Imperial	Metric	American
Damsons (or small blue plums)	2 lb	1 kg	2 lb
Apples	2 lb	1 kg	2 lb
Water			
Sugar			

Wipe the damsons and apples and cut them up without peeling, coring or stoning. Cover with water and boil for 20 minutes to a pulp. Put into a jelly bag, strain and measure the juice. Allow 1 lb/500 g/2 cups sugar to each pint/500 ml/2½ cups juice and warm the sugar. Bring the juice to the boil and stir in the sugar. Boil hard to setting point and pour into jars.

Green Gooseberry Mint Jelly

	Imperial	Metric	American
Green gooseberries	2 lb	1 kg	2 lb
Water			
Sugar			
Large mint sprigs	8	8	8

Wash the fruit and cover with cold water. Boil to a pulp and then strain through a jelly bag. Measure the juice and allow 1 lb/500 g/2 cups sugar to each pint/500 ml/2½ cups juice. Warm the sugar. Put the mint into the juice and boil for 3 minutes. Add the warm sugar and boil to setting point. Remove the mint and pour into jars. Use as a spread or serve with roast or grilled lamb.

Mrs Shenton's Elderberry Jelly

	Imperial	Metric	American
Elderberries	4 lb	2 kg	4 lb
Apples	2 lb	1 kg	2 lb
Water			
Sugar			

Remove the elderberries from their stems and put into a pan with the apples which have been cut up without peeling and coring. Cover with water and simmer until soft and juicy. Strain through a jelly bag and measure the juice. Allow 1 lb/500 g/2 cups sugar to each pint/500 ml/2½ cups juice, and warm the sugar. Bring the juice to the boil, stir in the sugar and boil hard to setting point. Pour into jars. This is a favourite North Country jelly and very cheap to make as there are always masses of elderberries in the hedgerows. We sometimes used to make it with crabapples (which were free as well), but then I liked to add the juice of 2 lemons when boiling the juice and sugar.

Mint Jelly

	Imperial	Metric	American
Apples	6 lb	3 kg	6 lb
Water	2 pints	1 litre	5 cups
Large bunch of fresh mint			
Lemon juice	1 tbsp	1 tbsp	1 tbsp
Sugar			
Green vegetable colouring			

Cut up the apples without peeling or coring them and boil in the water until soft. Strain through a jelly bag and measure the juice. Allow 1 lb/500 g/2 cups sugar to each pint/500 ml/2½ cups juice and warm the sugar. Heat the juice and stir in the warm sugar. Put half the mint into the mixture, with the lemon juice, and boil to setting point. Meanwhile, chop the remaining mint finely. When the jelly has reached setting point, remove the sprigs of mint. Stir in the chopped mint and a little colouring to give a bright, clear green. Put into small jars. Serve with roast or grilled lamb.

Lemon or Orange Jelly

	Imperial	Metric	American
Lemons or sweet oranges	1 lb	500 g	1 lb
Water	2 pints	1 litre	5 cups
Sugar			

Wipe the fruit and cut it into thin slices without peeling or removing the pips. Put into a bowl and pour over the water. Leave in a cool place to stand for 24 hours and then boil for 25 minutes. Leave to stand overnight and then boil again for 5 minutes. Strain through a jelly bag and measure the juice. Allow 1¼ lb/625 g/2½ cups sugar to each pint/500 ml/2½ cups juice, and warm the sugar. Bring the juice to the boil, stir in the warm sugar, boil hard to setting point. Pour into jars. This is a delicious spread for breakfast toast.

Redcurrant Jelly

Redcurrants
Water
Sugar

Wash the redcurrants and then just cover them with water. Boil for about 20 minutes until the juice is extracted. Strain through a jelly bag and measure the juice. Allow 1 lb/500 g/2 cups to each pint/500 ml/2½ cups juice and warm the sugar. Heat the juice, stir in the sugar and boil hard to setting point. Pour into small jars and serve with lamb or game.

Raspberry and Redcurrant Jelly

	Imperial	Metric	American
Raspberries	1½ lb	750 g	1½ lb
Redcurrants	1½ lb	750 g	1½ lb
Water	½ pint	250 ml	1¼ cups
Sugar			

Put the fruit into pan with the water and simmer for 15 minutes to release the juices. Strain through a jellybag and measure the juice. Allow 1 lb/500 g/2 cups sugar to each pint/500 ml/2½ cups juice, and warm the sugar. Bring the juice to the boil, stir in the sugar and boil hard to setting point. Pour into jars. The redcurrants make this jelly set firmly and the raspberries give it a lovely flavour.

Rowanberry Jelly

	Imperial	Metric	American
Apples	6 lb	3 kg	6 lb
Rowanberries	3 lb	1.5 kg	3 lb
Water			
Sugar			

Cut up the apples without peeling or coring. Put them into a pan with the berries and cold water to cover. Boil for 25 minutes to a pulp. Strain through a jelly bag. Measure the juice and allow 1 lb/500 g/2 cups sugar to each pint/500 ml/2½ cups juice. Warm the sugar. Heat the juice, stir in the sugar and boil hard to setting point. Pour into small jars, and serve as a spread, or with cold lamb, hare or venison.

Chapter Three

MARMALADES

These days, marmalades are usually made of citrus fruit, but the old "marmalade" was a thick purée of fruit and sugar which set to a firm paste, so quite a lot of old recipes include apples, pears and rhubarb among the ingredients. For citrus fruit marmalade, the fruit must be sliced, simmered in water until tender, and then boiled rapidly with sugar to setting point. Some people like to soak the peel overnight, although this is not necessary, but the peel must be thoroughly soft between the fingers before sugar is added. The water in the first cooking has to be evaporated, so usually the contents of the pan are reduced to about half for a good set.

When the peel is cut, it is important to save the pips and white pith which contain pectin and help the set of the marmalade. They should be tied in a piece of muslin and hung in the preserving pan during cooking, and removed before the sugar is added. The bag must be well squeezed on removal to extract all liquid.

When the sugar has been added to the hot fruit and disssolved gently, the mixture must be boiled quickly to setting point. It is ready when a little poured on to a cold plate sets and wrinkles when pushed with a finger. Always cool marmalade slightly before potting, and stir well to prevent peel rising in the jars. Cover in the same way as jam.

Apple Marmalade

	Imperial	Metric	American
Apples	2 lb	1 kg	2 lb
Mixed candied peel	8 oz	225 g	2¼ cups
Water	½ pint	250 ml	1¼ cups
Juice of oranges	2	2	2
Sugar	1½ lb	750 g	3 cups

Peel and core the apples and cut them into small pieces about the size of a marble. Mince the peel and simmer it in the water for 5 minutes. Add the apples and the orange juice and simmer until the apples are soft. Stir in the warm sugar and then boil hard for 10 minutes. Test for setting; then stir well and put into jars.

Cottage Marmalade

	Imperial	Metric	American
Rhubarb	1 lb	500 g	1 lb
Oranges	3	3	3
Sugar	1 lb	500 g	2 cups

Cut the rhubarb into small pieces. Grate the orange rind and add to the rhubarb. Remove the pith from the oranges and take out pips. Tie pith and pips into a piece of muslin. Cut the oranges in crosswise slices and cut each slice in quarters. Put the orange pieces with the rhubarb and grated rind and just cover with water. Simmer for 20 minutes until the fruit is soft and then remove the bag of pips. Stir in the warm sugar and then boil rapidly to setting point. Stir well and pour into jars.

Grapefruit and Apple Marmalade

	Imperial	Metric	American
Grapefruit	2	2	2
Water	1½ pints	750 ml	3¾ cups
Apples	1½ lb	750 g	5 cups
Sugar	2 lb	1 kg	4 cups

Cut the grapefruit in half and squeeze out the juice into a bowl. Remove the pips and scrape off the white pith from the skins. Put the pips and pith into a piece of muslin and tie on to the handle of the preserving pan. Mince the grapefruit skins and mix with the juice and water. Leave to stand overnight. Put into the pan and boil for 30 minutes. Peel and core the apples and cut them into small pieces. Add to the grapefruit mixture and cook for 15 minutes. Remove the bag of pips and pith. Stir in the warm sugar until dissolved and boil rapidly to setting point. Stir well and pour into jars.

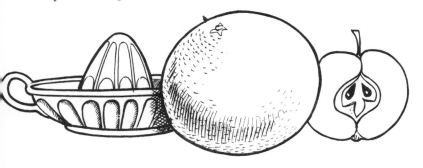

Pear Marmalade

	Imperial	Metric	American
Pears	4 lb	2 kg	4 lb
Sugar	4 lb	2 kg	8 cups
Lemons	2	2	2
Oranges	3	3	3

Put all the fruit through the mincer. Don't peel the pears; only core them. They should be rather green and firm. Put into the preserving pan with sugar and stir gently over low heat. When the sugar has dissolved, bring to the boil and boil rapidly until thick and a little sets on a plate. Put into warm jars. I made this using William pears as soon as they were picked, over two years ago. We are eating the last of it now, and it's excellent. The recipe came from British Columbia, and sometimes the oranges are left out and 8 oz/225 g/1½ cups minced crystallised ginger is stirred in just before potting instead, and this makes a really tasty preserve which will keep for years.

Sadberge Marmalade

	Imperial	Metric	American
Seville oranges	8	8	8
Sweet oranges	4	4	4
Lemons	2	2	2
Water	8 pints	5 litres	20 cups
Sugar			

Put the skins from all the fruit through the mincer and put this pulp in the water. Leave to stand for 24 hours. Cut the fruit into dice, taking out the pips, and put the fruit with the skins. Put the pips into a muslin bag. Boil together for 45 minutes, and then take out the bag of pips. Measure the pulp and allow 1 lb/500 g/2 cups sugar to each pint/500 ml/2½ cups pulp. Warm the sugar slightly in the oven and then stir into the pulp. Stir over low heat until the sugar is completely dissolved, and then boil fast to a set. Put into warm jars. A good, tasty marmalade.

Orange Marmalade

	Imperial	Metric	American
Seville oranges	2 lb	1 kg	2 lb
Lemons	2	2	2
Water	5 pints	2.5 litres	12½ cups
Sugar	9 lb	4.25 kg	18 cups

Cut up the oranges and lemons in small pieces, cover with water and leave to stand overnight. Put the pips into a muslin bag and suspend in the pan. Simmer the fruit and water until the skins are soft and the contents of the pan reduced to half. Add the warm sugar and stir in until dissolved, then boil hard to setting point. Leave to stand for 10 minutes, stir well and pour into jars. I like to mince the skins for this marmalade and always get a clear bright marmalade.

Rhubarb Marmalade

	Imperial	Metric	American
Lemons	5	5	5
Rhubarb	4 lb	2 kg	4 lb
Almond essence	2 tsp	10 ml	2 tsp
Ginger essence	2 tbsp	30 ml	2 tbsp
Sugar	6 lb	3 kg	12 cups

Grate the rind from 3 lemons and put into a pan with ½ pint/250 ml/1¼ cups water, the juice of the lemons, the chopped rhubarb, the essences and the sugar. Stir together over low heat until the sugar dissolves, then boil fast to setting point. Put into warm jars. Keep for a month before using. We use this as marmalade for toast, but it makes good tarts too, or a filling for a sandwich cake.

Green Tomato Marmalade

	Imperial	Metric	American
Green tomatoes	4 lb	2 kg	4 lb
Lemons	5	5	5
Water	¼ pint	125 ml	½ cup
Sugar	2 lb	1 kg	4 cups

Cut up the tomatoes. Peel the lemons and cut the flesh into thin slices. Mix the tomatoes and lemons together with the water and heat slowly to the boil. Boil for 10 minutes, then stir in the sugar. Stir over low heat until the sugar has dissolved, then boil rapidly to setting point. Put into warm jars. A layer of this baked between two crusts makes a useful bite for tea-time.

Trinity Marmalade

	Imperial	Metric	American
Grapefruit	2	2	2
Lemons	3	3	3
Oranges	3	3	3
Water			
Sugar			

Cut the fruit in half and squeeze out the juice. Put the pips into a muslin bag. Mince the peel and the pulp. Put the minced peel and pulp, juice and bag of pips into a bowl and cover with cold water, allowing 3 pints/1.5 litres/7½ cups water to each pint/500 ml/2½ cups pulp. Leave to stand for 2 nights. Measure the mixture and allow 1 lb/500 g/2 cups sugar to each pint/500 ml/2½ cups pulp. Boil the pulp for 20 minutes, then add the warm sugar and stir well until the sugar has dissolved. Boil fast to setting point and pour into warm jars. I've left this to stand as long as 5 days and it has turned out a lovely, tasty jellied preserve, with no hard pieces of peel in it.

Chapter Four

BOTTLING

Fruit and tomatoes are the most successful items for bottling, but it is not recommended to bottle vegetables, meat or poultry at home. Successful bottling depends on heating fruit enough, closing the jars while they are hot, and using airtight jars. Preserving jars may have glass or metal lids which rest on a rubber band, and either clips or screwbands are used to hold the lids tightly in place when the jars are cooling. When the jars are cold, the vacuum formed inside holds the lid in place. Always use clean jars and lids without ridges or chips, and be sure that rubber bands are soft and flexible if they are not attached to the lids.

Fruit should be carefully prepared for bottling and should be ripe, but not over-ripe. Unsound fruit, stalks and leaves must be removed, and the fruit rinsed in clean cold water. Gooseberries should be topped and tailed and pricked to prevent shrivelling. Raspberries should be free from maggots, but are better not rinsed. Rhubarb needs wiping and cutting into short lengths.

Stone fruit should be just ripe and rinsed in clean cold water. Large fruit may be halved and stoned, and peaches should be skinned. Fruit with light-coloured flesh should be covered with syrup or water as soon as possible to prevent discolouration. Hard fruit, such as apples and pears, are usually peeled, cored and cut into slices or halves, but apples may also be made into purée. Tomatoes may be bottled whole if small, or they can be cut into halves or quarters, or prepared as purée.

Fruit may be bottled in water or syrup, but

syrup keeps a better flavour and also means that fruit is ready for use without further prepartion. Usually a proportion of 1 lb/500 g/2 cups sugar to 2 pints/1 litre/5 cups water gives a suitable strength syrup for most fruit. Sugar and water should be boiled for 1 minute before use (either hot or cold according to method).

The two easiest bottling methods are in a slow water bath, or in a moderate oven.

Slow Water Bath

A deep container such as a fish kettle or preserving pan should be used, with a false bottom so that jars are not in direct contact with the base of the pan. The bottles should be filled with fruit and cold syrup or water, and then the rings, lids and clips put on. Screwbands should be fitted on but unscrewed by a quarter-turn during processing. Cover the jars in the pan with cold water and raise the temperature gradually to reach the given temperature in 90 minutes. The water should then be maintained at that temperature for the required time, before being removed and the screwbands tightened and the jars left to cool.

Goosberries for pies, pie-rhubarb and apple slices should be maintained at 165°F/85°C for 10 minutes. Tightly packed dessert gooseberries, dessert rhubarb, whole stone-fruit, apples, peaches and halved plums should be maintained at 180°F/90°C for 15 minutes. Pears and whole tomatoes should be maintained at 190°F/95°C for 30 minutes.

Moderate Oven Method

For this oven method, put the bottles on pads of newspaper or a solid block of wood so that the glass does not touch hot metal. Preheat the oven for 15 minutes to 300°F/150°C/Gas Mark 2. Pack in fruit and add boiling water or syrup and adjust rings and lids, but screwbands should not be put on. Allow longer time for processing for larger quantities of bottles. For pie-gooseberries, pie-rhubarb and apple slices, allow 30—40 minutes for 1—4 lb/.5—2 kg (45—60 minutes for 5—10 lb/2.5—5 kg). Tightly packed dessert gooseberries, dessert rhubarb and whole stone fruit need 40—50 minutes for 1—4 lb/.5—2 kg (75—90 minutes for 5—10 lb/2.5—5 kg). Screwbands should be put on immediately the jars are taken from the oven.

When jars are quite cold the day after processing, the clips or screwbands should be removed and each jar carefully lifted by the lid. If it remains firm, a vacuum has formed, but if the lid comes off the jar has not sealed properly and the fruit will not keep. It may be re-processed; otherwise the fruit should be used up immediately. The screwbands should be washed and dried thoroughly and rubbed with a little oil inside before being put on loosely for storage, but spring clips should never be stored on the bottles. Keep fruit in a cool dry place away from sunlight, and label the jars carefully so that they are used in rotation.

Chapter Five

PICKLES

Vinegar, sugar, salt and spices are essential for these pickles which are not difficult to make. Put the pickles into preserving jars or into screwtop jars with vinegar-proof lids, as paper lids will allow the vinegar to evaporate. Use packets of pickling spice from the chemist or grocer and malt vinegar and make your own spiced vinegar by boiling the spices in the vinegar for 10 minutes before use. A ready-spiced pickling vinegar can now be bought which saves a little time. Always use block cooking salt for pickling and not the free-running variety which contains chemicals.

Cabbage Pickle

	Imperial	Metric	American
Hard cabbage	1	1	1
Onions	1 lb	500 g	2½ cups
Kitchen salt	4 oz	100 g	8 tbsp
Vinegar	3 pints	1.5 litres	7½ cups
Plain flour	2 oz	50 g	½ cup
Sugar	12 oz	350 g	1½ cups
Curry powder	2 tsp	2 tsp	2 tsp
Mustard powder	2 tsbp	2 tbsp	2 tbsp

Shred the cabbage and cut the onions in thin rings. Put into a bowl, sprinkle with salt and leave overnight. Drain off salty liquid. Put into a pan with 2 pints/1 litre/5 cups vinegar and boil gently for 20 minutes. Mix flour, sugar, curry powder, mustard and remaining vinegar. Stir into the cabbage and boil hard for 5 minutes. Put into jars and cover.

Pickled Cherries

	Imperial	Metric	American
Glacé cherries			
Vinegar	1 pint	500 ml	2½ cups
Salt	1 saltsp	1 saltsp	1 saltsp
Pickling spice	1 oz	25 g	2 tbsp

Fill small jars with the cherries. Put the vinegar, salt and spice into a pan and boil for 5 minutes. Strain over the cherries and cover. Be sure the cherries are really well covered in the vinegar, as they do soak it up. Keep for about 4 months before using. This sounds unusual, but they are very good, particularly with ham or chicken.

Fig Pickle

	Imperial	Metric	American
Dried figs	1 lb	500 g	1 lb
Sugar	1 lb	500 g	2 cups
Vinegar	½ pint	250 ml	1¼ cups
Ground cloves	1 tsp	1 tsp	1 tsp
Ground mace	½ tsp	½ tsp	½ tsp
Mustard powder	1 tsp	1 tsp	1 tsp

Soak the figs overnight in cold water to cover and then drain thoroughly. Put the other ingredients into a pan and heat slowly, stirring well to dissolve the sugar. Add the figs and then simmer for 1 hour. Put into small jars and cover.

Pickled Damsons

	Imperial	Metric	American
Damsons	6 lb	3 kg	6 lb
Vinegar	1½ pints	750 ml	3¾ cups
Sugar	4 lb	2 kg	8 cups
Pickling spice	1 oz	25 g	2 tbsp
Cloves	6	6	6

Wipe the damsons, prick them with a needle, and put into a bowl. Put the vinegar and sugar into a pan and add the spice and cloves tied into a piece of muslin. Boil together for 5 minutes and pour over the fruit. Leave to stand for 24 hours. Drain off the juice, bring to the boil and pour over the fruit. Leave to stand for 24 hours. Take out the spice bag, and put the fruit and juice into a pan. Bring slowly to the boil without breaking the fruit. Lift out the fruit with a slotted spoon and put into jars. Bring the liquid to the boil, pour over the damsons and cover. Cherries can be pickled in the same way.

Pickled French Beans

	Imperial	Metric	American
French beans			
Vinegar	1 pint	500 ml	2½ cups
Pickling spice	1 oz	25 g	2 tbsp
Salt	1 tsp	1 tsp	1 tsp

String the beans and cut them into 1 in/2.5 cm chunks. Boil until tender in salted water. Drain and put into jars. Boil the vinegar and spice for 3 minutes and then stir in the salt. Leave until cold and pour over the beans to cover them well. Cover and keep for 2 months before using. In the summer, I make up quite a large quantity of spiced vinegar. When we have beans for a meal, I cook an extra lot and when they are cold they go into jars to be covered with the prepared vinegar, so I don't have to waste any time on pickling them specially.

Pickled Leeks

	Imperial	Metric	American
Medium-sized leeks			
Vinegar	1 pint	500 ml	2½ cups
Pickling spice	1 oz	25 g	2 tbsp
Salt	1 tsp	1 tsp	1 tsp
Sugar	1 tsp	1 tsp	1 tsp

We love eating leeks in the North of England and steam them to serve plain as a vegetable, or cover them with white sauce. For this recipe, they need to be sliced across in thick slices and steamed until barely cooked, then cooled.

Prepare the vinegar by boiling it for 5 minutes with the spice, salt and sugar. Take out the spices and pour the vinegar over the leeks packed into small jars. Keep for 2 or 3 weeks before using.

Pickled Green Walnuts

	Imperial	Metric	American
Green walnuts			
Water	2 pints	1 litre	5 cups
Salt	8 oz	225 g	16 tbsp
Vinegar	2 pints	1 litre	5 cups
Pickling spice	1 oz	25 g	2 tbsp
Mustard powder	1 tbsp	1 tbsp	1 tbsp

Use the walnuts in June or early July while the kernels are still very soft and the outer casings are bright green and firm. Be prepared to get your hands stained brown as walnut juice makes rather a mess. Prick the green casing of the walnuts all over with a fork. Boil the water and salt together and pour over the walnuts. Soak the walnuts in the salted water for 5 days. Drain them and put them on wooden racks spread out in the sun to turn black, turning them over often. Boil the vinegar, spice and mustard powder for 10 minutes and take out the spices. Pack the black walnuts into jars and pour over the vinegar. Cover and keep for at least 2 weeks before using.

Pickled Nasturtiums

	Imperial	Metric	American
Nasturtium seeds			
Vinegar	1 pint	500 ml	2½ cups
Salt	1 oz	25 g	2 tbsp
Pickling spice	1 oz	25 g	2 tbsp

Gather the nasturtium seeds on a dry day, when they are young and soft. Boil together the vinegar, salt and spice (tied in a bag) for 5 minutes. Put the vinegar into a preserving jar. Wipe the nasturtium seeds and drop them into the vinegar. Keep covered and add seeds from time to time and screw on the lid again. Prepare the pickle one year for use the next. These hot, spicy seeds are used as a substitute for capers in sauce to go with boiled mutton, and in fish dishes and salads. Just lift them out of the jar and drain them well before use.

Mustard Pickle

	Imperial	Metric	American
Onions	4 lb	2 kg	4 lb
Cauliflowers	3	3	3
Water	8 pints	5 litre	20 cups
Salt	1 lb	500 g	32 tbsp
Vinegar	1½ pints	750 ml	3¾ cups
Sugar	8 oz	225 g	1 cup
Mustard powder	1 tbsp	1 tbsp	1 tbsp
Plain flour	2 oz	50 g	½ cup
Turmeric	1 tbsp	1 tbsp	1 tbsp

Some small green tomatoes, a little celery, and French beans can be added to the vegetables if liked, and a small cucumber, is good, too. Cut the vegetables into neat small pieces. Boil the water and salt and leave until cold. Pour over the vegetables and leave to stand for 36 hours. Mix together the vinegar, sugar, mustard, flour and turmeric and bring to the boil. Drain the vegetables and add to the vinegar mixture. Bring to the boil and then simmer for 15 minutes. Pour into jars and cover.

Mixed Pickle

	Imperial	Metric	American
Cauliflower			
French beans			
Small onions			
Marrow			
Cucumber			
Vinegar	2 pints	1 litre	5 cups
Root ginger	½ oz	15 g	½ tbsp
Salt	1 tbsp	1 tbsp	1 tbsp
Water	2 pints	1 litre	5 cups

Use a mixture of vegetables, according to what you have in the garden, to give 2—3 lb/1—1.5 kg weight. Cut the cauliflower into sprigs. String the beans and cut them into small chunks. Peel and dice onion, marrow and cucumber. Put the vinegar, spice and ginger into a pan and simmer for 20 minutes, strain and cool. Bring the salt and water to the boil and put in the prepared vegetables. Bring to the boil and simmer for 3 minutes. Drain well, put into jars, cover with vinegar and seal.

Prune Pickle

	Imperial	Metric	American
Dried prunes			
Vinegar	2 pints	1 litre	5 cups
Pickling spice	1 oz	25 g	2 tbsp

Use good quality plump prunes, wash them well and put them into small screwtop jars. Simmer the vinegar and spice for 8 minutes and remove the spice. Pour the boiling vinegar over the prunes to cover them well, and cover. Leave for about 6 months before using with cold pork or ham.

Pickled Red Cabbage

	Imperial	Metric	American
Red cabbage	1	1	1
Cooking salt			
Vinegar	1 pint	500 ml	2½ cups
Pickling spice	1 oz	25 g	2 tbsp
Mustard powder	1 tsp	1 tsp	1 tsp

Cut the cabbage heart into four pieces and take out the centre stalk. Shred the cabbage pieces finely and put on to a large flat dish and sprinkle lightly with salt. Leave to stand for 24 hours and then drain very thoroughly. Pack into jars. Boil vinegar, pickling spice and mustard for 5 minutes and leave until cold. Pour over the cabbage and cover. Do not use the vinegar hot or it will make the cabbage blue and soft.

Pickled Onions or Shallots

	Imperial	Metric	American
Small onions or shallots			
Salt	8 oz	225 g	16 tbsp
Water	4 pints	2 litres	10 cups
Vinegar	2 pints	1 litre	5 cups
Pickling spice	1 oz	25 g	2 tbsp
Sugar	2 tsp	2 tsp	2 tsp

Pour boiling water over the small onions or shallots and peel them. Boil the salt and water, cool and pour over the onions. Let them stand for 2 days and drain. Pack into jars. Boil the vinegar and spice for 5 minutes and leave until cold. Pour over the onions or shallots and add 1 teaspoon sugar to each jar. Cover and leave for one month before using.

Chapter Six

CHUTNEY

Chutney is one of the nicest kitchen preserves and you can make it from all sorts of odds and ends of fruit and vegetables. Vinegar and sugar act as preservatives and dried fruit and spices add a special flavour. Do be sure to cook the chutney long enough so that it is rich and brown and as thick as jam. Pot it in clean jars and cover tightly with vinegar-proof screwtop or plastic lids. Paper covers will allow the vinegar to evaporate and the chutney will become dark and dry. Store it in a cool dark place, and you will find it tastes better if kept for a few months so that the flavours blend and mature.

Apple Chutney

	Imperial	Metric	American
Cooking apples	1 lb	500 g	1 lb
Sultanas	8 oz	225 g	1 cup
Shallots or small onions	6 oz	175 g	6
Ground ginger	1 tsp	1 tsp	1 tsp
Sugar	7 oz	200 g	3/4—1 cup
Salt	3 tsp	3 tsp	3 tsp
Vinegar	1 pint	500 ml	2½ cups

Peel and core the apples and chop them finely. Put with the sultanas. Peel and chop the shallots or onions finely. Mix all the ingredients together and leave to stand for 1 hour. Simmer until thick and brown, stirring often to prevent burning. Fill jars and cover. The men used to call this "Hot and Sweet", and I made it with hard green windfalls.

Bishopton Chutney

	Imperial	Metric	American
Cooking apples	2 lb	1 kg	2 lb
Seedless raisins	1 lb	500 g	3 cups
Garlic	4 oz	100 g	¼ lb
Sugar	1 lb	500 g	2 cups
Vinegar	1 pint	500 ml	2½ cups
Salt	1 tsp	1 tsp	1 tsp
Ground ginger	½ tsp	½ tsp	½ tsp
Pinch of pepper			

Peel and chop the apples finely. Add to the chopped raisins and finely sliced garlic. Stir in the remaining ingredients. Bring to the boil, stirring well, and then simmer until brown and thick. Fill jars and cover.

Apple and Red Tomato Chutney

	Imperial	Metric	American
Cooking apples	3 lb	1.5 kg	3 lb
Red tomatoes	3 lb	1.5 kg	3 lb
Onions	1 lb	500 g	1 lb
Sugar	1 lb	500 g	2 cups
Ground ginger	1 tsp	1 tsp	1 tsp
Vinegar	2 pints	1 litre	5 cups
Salt	2 oz	50 g	4 tbsp
Pickling spice	1 oz	25 g	2 tbsp

Peel and cut up the apples, tomatoes and onions and put them into a pan with the sugar and ginger. In a separate pan, put the vinegar, salt and the pickling spice tied into a muslin bag. Bring to the boil and boil for 3 minutes. Take out the spice bag. Pour the vinegar over the other ingredients and simmer until thick and brown, stirring well. Fill jars and cover.

Banana Chutney

	Imperial	Metric	American
Bananas	16	16	16
Onions	2 lb	1 kg	2 lb
Dates	1 lb	500 g	2½ cups
Crystallised ginger	8 oz	225 g	1½ cups
Salt	1 tbsp	1 tbsp	1 tbsp
Pickling spice	1 oz	25 g	2 tbsp
Vinegar	2 pints	1 litre	5 cups
Sugar	1 lb	500 g	2 cups

Peel and slice the bananas and put into a pan. Add the finely chopped onions, minced dates and ginger, and salt. Put the pickling spice into a bag and hang in the pan. Add the vinegar, bring to the boil and boil for 5 minutes. Take out the spice bag. Stir in the sugar and simmer over low heat until rich and brown. This is one of our special favourites and it is really delicious.

Gooseberry Chutney

	Imperial	Metric	American
Green gooseberries	2 lb	1 kg	2 lb
Mixed candied peel	8 oz	225 g	2 cups
Sultanas	1 lb	500 g	3 cups
Garlic	1 oz	25 g	1 tbsp
Salt	4 oz	100 g	8 tbsp
Sugar	1 lb	500 g	2 cups
Pepper	1 tsp	1 tsp	1 tsp
Crystallised ginger	2 oz	50 g	½ cup
Curry powder	1 tbsp	1 tbsp	1 tbsp
Onions	1 lb	500 g	2½ cups
Vinegar	2 pints	1 litre	5 cups

Top and tail the gooseberries and put them into a pan. Add the chopped peel and whole sultanas. Stir in chopped garlic, salt, sugar, pepper, chopped ginger and curry powder. Peel and chop the onions finely and add to the other ingredients. Bring to the boil, stirring well, and then simmer until brown and thick. Fill jars and cover.

No-Cook Date Chutney

	Imperial	Metric	American
Pickling spice	1 oz	25 g	2 tbsp
Vinegar	1 pint	500 ml	2½ cups
Dates	2 lb	1 kg	2½ cups
Crystallised ginger	1 lb	500 g	4 cups
Mustard powder	2 tsp	2 tsp	2 tsp
Golden syrup	6 tbsp	6 tbsp	6 tbsp

Put the spice into a muslin bag and add to the vinegar in a pan. Boil together for 7 minutes. Add minced dates and minced ginger, mustard and syrup and stir thoroughly. Leave to stand until cool and stir again. Fill jars and cover.

Green Plum Chutney

	Imperial	Metric	American
Stoned unripe plums	4 lb	2 kg	4 lb
Large onions	2	2	2
Seedless raisins	1 lb	500 g	3 cups
Sugar	1 lb	500 g	2 cups
Cooking apples	1 lb	500 g	1 lb
Salt	3 tsp	3 tsp	3 tsp
Pepper	1 tsp	1 tsp	1 tsp
Ground ginger	½ oz	15 g	1 tbsp
Mustard seed	½ oz	15 g	1 tbsp
Vinegar	1 pint	500 ml	2½ cups
Pickling spice	1 oz	25 g	2 tbsp

Use green unripe plums and stone them before weighing. Cut up the plums and chop the onions finely. Mix with the raisins, sugar, chopped apples, salt, pepper, ginger and mustard. Boil the vinegar and spice together for 6 minutes and remove the spice. Pour the spiced vinegar over the other ingredients and simmer gently until brown and thick. Fill jars and cover. This is a good chutney to make when a tree is laden with plums which may not all ripen. Pick off the plumpest and cut the soft green flesh off the stones for making the chutney.

Lanchester Chutney

	Imperial	Metric	American
Cooking apples	3 lb	1.5 kg	3 lb
Large onions	3	3	3
Large tomatoes	4	4	4
Sultanas	12 oz	350 g	2½ cups
Soy sauce	1 tbsp	1 tbsp	1 tbsp
Salad oil	2 tbsp	2 tbsp	2 tbsp
Salt	3 tsp	3 tsp	3 tsp
Ground ginger	1 tsp	1 tsp	1 tsp
Anchovy essence	1 tsp	1 tsp	1 tsp
Pepper	1 saltsp	1 saltsp	1 saltsp
Mustard seed	¼ oz	6 g	1 tsp
Vinegar	½ pint	250 ml	1¼ cups

Peel, core and chop the apples finely. Peel and chop the onions and tomatoes. Put all the ingredients into a pan and simmer very gently until thick and brown. Fill jars and cover.

Green Tomato Chutney

	Imperial	Metric	American
Green tomatoes	4 lb	2 kg	4 lb
Cooking apples	2 lb	1 kg	2 lb
Shallots or small onions	1 lb	500 g	1 lb
Dates	1 lb	500 g	2½ cups
Vinegar	3 pints	1.5 litres	7½ cups
Golden syrup	2 lb	1 kg	3 cups
Mustard powder	½ oz	15 g	½ tbsp
Salt	3 tbsp	3 tbsp	3 tbsp
Pepper	2 tsp	2 tsp	2 tsp

Cut the tomatoes in small pieces without peeling. Peel and core the apples and cut them in pieces. Peel and chop the shallots or onions, and chop the dates. Put the shallots or onions into a pan with the vinegar and simmer until they are soft. Add the remaining ingredients and simmer for about 1 hour until thick and brown. Fill jars and cover. I like to use golden syrup for sweetening sometimes as it has a very distinctive flavour.

Mrs Latchem's Chutney

	Imperial	Metric	American
Cooking apples	2 lb	1 kg	2 lb
Onions	8 oz	225 g	1½ cups
Sultanas	8 oz	225 g	1½ cups
Mustard seed	1 oz	25 g	1 tbsp
Salt	2 oz	50 g	4 tbsp
Pepper	½ tsp	½ tsp	½ tsp
Sugar	8 oz	225 g	1 cup
Vinegar	1½ pints	750 ml	3¾ cups
Ground ginger	1 oz	25 g	1 tbsp

Peel and core the apples and cut into pieces. Peel the onions and chop them finely. Put all the ingredients into a pan and bring to the boil. Simmer until thick and brown. Fill jars and cover. If you do not like much ginger, only put in half the amount and taste when the chutney is finished. You can always add more if you like. Mrs Latchem had a big orchard at Redworth and during the 1914 War she made big quantities of this chutney. People came from far and wide to buy it.

Orange Chutney

	Imperial	Metric	American
Cooking apples	3 lb	1.5kg	3 lb
Peeled oranges	8 oz	225 g	1½ cups
Dates	1½ lb	750 g	3¾ cups
Red tomatoes	1½ lb	750 g	1½ lb
Sugar	3 lb	1.5 kg	6 cups
Vinegar	6 pints	4 litres	15 cups
Chillies	2 oz	50 g	¼ cup
Salt	1 tbsp	1 tbsp	1 tbsp

Peel, core and chop the apples and mix with the oranges cut in dice (don't use the orange peel). Add minced dates and sliced tomatoes. Add the sugar, vinegar, chopped chillies and salt and bring to the boil. Simmer until thick and brown. Fill jars and cover. The chillies make this a hot chutney, and may be omitted if you like, but then it is good to put in a little ground ginger instead.

Mixed Autumn Chutney

	Imperial	Metric	American
Pears	2 lb	1 kg	2 lb
Apples	2 lb	1 kg	2 lb
Onions	1 lb	500 g	1 lb
Dates	1 lb	500 g	2½ cups
Vinegar	2 pints	1 litre	5 cups
Pickling spice	1 oz	25 g	2 tbsp
Salt	2 tbsp	2 tbsp	2 tbsp
Mustard powder	2 tbsp	2 tbsp	2 tbsp
Ground ginger	1 oz	25 g	2 tbsp
Golden syrup	2 lb	1 kg	3 cups

Peel and core the pears and apples and cut them in small pieces. Peel and chop the onions, and chop the dates. Put the vinegar into a pan with the pickling spice tied in a bag. Add the salt, mustard, ginger and syrup and boil together for 5 minutes. Remove the spice bag. Put in the pears, apples, onions and dates and simmer together until thick and brown. Fill jars and cover.

Newton Apple Chutney

	Imperial	Metric	American
Apples	4 lb	2 kg	4 lb
Ripe tomatoes	1 lb	500 g	1 lb
Onions	1 lb	500 g	1 lb
Sultanas	1 lb	500 g	3 cups
Vinegar	3 pints	1.5 litres	7½ cups
Golden syrup	2 lb	1 kg	3 cups
Salt	4 tsp	4 tsp	4 tsp
Mustard powder	1 tsp	1 tsp	1 tsp
Ground ginger	½ oz	15 g	1 tbsp
Lemon	2	2	2

Peel, core and cut up the apples. Peel and cut up the tomatoes. Peel the onions and chop them finely. Put apples, tomatoes and onions into a pan with the vinegar and boil until the onions are soft. Add syrup, salt, mustard, ginger, and grated rind and juice of the lemons. Boil until thick and brown. This is a mild and useful chutney which is good with any kind of meat. It can also be heated to serve as a good apple sauce with pork or sausages.

Peggy's Pear Chutney

	Imperial	Metric	American
Pears	4 lb	2 kg	4 lb
Onions	1 lb	500 g	1 lb
Salt	2 tbsp	2 tbsp	2 tbsp
Sugar	1½ lb	750 g	3 cups
Ground ginger	1 oz	25 g	1 tbsp
Dates	1 lb	500 g	2 cups
Sultanas	8 oz	225 g	1 cup
Mustard powder	1 tbsp	1 tbsp	1 tbsp
Vinegar	2 pints	1 litre	2½ cups

Peel, core and chop the pears. Peel the onions and chop them finely. Put into a pan with the salt, sugar, ginger, chopped dates, sultanas, mustard and vinegar. Bring to the boil and then simmer until thick and brown. Fill jars and cover. Boiling time will depend on the ripeness of the pears. I have made this with parts of the big ripe pears which get blown off the tree and it has proved a real favourite.

Stanhope Rhubarb Chutney

	Imperial	Metric	American
Rhubarb	2 lb	1 kg	2 lb
Sultanas	1 lb	500 g	3 cups
Soft brown sugar	2 lb	1 kg	2 lb
Large onion	1	1	1
Salt	1 oz	25 g	2 tbsp
Ground ginger	1 oz	25 g	2 tbsp
Pepper	½ tsp	½ tsp	½ tsp
Lemons	2	2	2
Vinegar	1 pint	500 ml	2½ cups

Cut the rhubarb into small pieces. Put into a pan with the sultanas, sugar and chopped onion. Add the salt, ginger and pepper. Peel the lemons and remove the pips. Cut the lemon flesh into small pieces and add to the other ingredients. Pour in the vinegar and bring to the boil. Stir well and simmer until brown and thick. Fill jars and cover. This is a great favourite and we make it every year.

Thornton-Le-Dale Chutney

	Imperial	Metric	American
Apples	4 lb	2 kg	4 lb
Ripe tomatoes	2 lb	1 kg	2 lb
Onions	2 lb	1 kg	2 lb
Sugar	1½ lb	750 g	3 cups
Salt	2 tbsp	2 tbsp	2 tbsp
Pepper	1 oz	25 g	2 tbsp
Ground ginger	2 tbsp	2 tbsp	2 tbsp
Mustard seed	½ oz	15 g	1 tbsp
Raisins	1 lb	500 g	3 cups
Vinegar	2 pints	1 litre	5 cups

Peel the apples, tomatoes and onions and mince them all together. Add all the other ingredients and simmer until thick and brown. Fill jars and cover. This is a favourite in rural Yorkshire and sells well in 'bring and buy' sales.

Rhubarb Chutney

	Imperial	Metric	American
Rhubarb	1½ lb	750 g	1½ lb
Onions	1½ lb	750 g	1½ lb
Garlic	4 oz	100 g	¼ lb
Vinegar	1 pint	500 ml	2½ cups
Sugar	1 lb	500 g	2 cups
Salt	1 tsp	1 tsp	1 tsp
Pepper	½ tsp	½ tsp	½ tsp
Ground cloves	½ tsp	½ tsp	½ tsp

Cut the rhubarb, onions and garlic into small pieces. Add the vinegar and boil for 15 minutes. Add the remaining ingredients and simmer for about 1 hour until thick and brown. Fill jars and cover.

Tomato and Onion Chutney

	Imperial	Metric	American
Ripe tomatoes	3 lb	1.5 kg	3 lb
Onions	1 lb	500 g	1 lb
Salt	1½ tbsp	1½ tbsp	1½ tbsp
Vinegar	2 pints	1 litre	5 cups
Sugar	1 lb	500 g	2 cups
Mustard powder	1 oz	25 g	4 tbsp
Pickling spice	1 oz	25 g	2 tbsp

Peel and slice the tomatoes and onions. Sprinkle with salt and leave to stand overnight. Add vinegar, sugar and mustard and bring to the boil. Put the spice into a muslin bag and hang it in the pan. After the mixture has boiled for 5 minutes take out the spice bag. Continue simmering until the chutney is thick and brown. Fill jars and cover.

Red Tomato Chutney

	Imperial	Metric	American
Ripe tomatoes	1 lb	500 g	1 lb
Cooking apples	1 lb	500 g	1 lb
Onions	8 oz	225 g	1½ cups
Sultanas	8 oz	225 g	2 cups
Crystallised ginger	8 oz	225 g	2 cups
Salt	1 tsp	1 tsp	1 tsp
Chillies	12	12	12
Sugar	8 oz	225 g	1 cup
Vinegar	1 pint	500 ml	2½ cups

Peel the tomatoes, apples and onions and mince them with the sultanas, ginger and chillies. Put all the ingredients into a pan, bring to the boil and then simmer until thick and brown. Fill jars and cover. The chillies make this chutney quite hot, so they can be left out if you like.

Marrow Chutney

	Imperial	Metric	American
Large marrow	1	1	1
Cooking salt	2 oz	50 g	2 tbsp
Vinegar	2 pints	1 litre	5 cups
Mustard powder	1 tbsp	1 tbsp	1 tbsp
Turmeric	½ oz	15 g	2 tbsp
Ground ginger	1 oz	25 g	4 tbsp
Sugar	4 oz	100 g	½ cup
Large onions	2	2	2

Peel the marrow and cut it into dice. Weigh out 3 lb/1.5 kg/7½ cups flesh. Sprinkle with the salt and leave to stand for 24 hours. Drain off the liquid and put the marrow into a pan. Mix together the vinegar, mustard, turmeric, ginger and sugar and add to the pan. Add the finely chopped onions. Bring to the boil and then simmer until thick and brown. Fill jars and cover.

Chapter Seven

DRESSINGS, SAUCES AND KETCHUPS

We make a lot of different sauces and ketchups to use in the winter months; quite often I just sieve my chutney mixtures and bottle those. It is best to put sauces into sterilised sauce bottles with screwtop vinegarproof lids, and then the bottles should be heated in a sterilising water bath in the same way as bottled fruit (see page 42). These days, it's quite a good idea to freeze the fruit sauces in small containers, which saves the bother of sterilising them.

Apple Sauce

	Imperial	Metric	American
Apples	*4 lb*	*2 kg*	*4 lb*
Vinegar	*2 pints*	*1 litre*	*5 cups*
Onions	*8 oz*	*225 g*	*1½ cups*
Dates	*8 oz*	*225 g*	*1¼ cups*
Salt	*2 oz*	*50 g*	*4 tbsp*
Ground ginger	*1 oz*	*25 g*	*4 tbsp*
Golden syrup	*2 lb*	*1 kg*	*3 cups*

Cut the apples small without peeling them. Put into a pan with the vinegar, finely chopped onions, chopped dates, salt and ginger. Simmer until the apples and onions are soft and then stir in the syrup. Continue cooking until the mixture is thick and then put through a sieve. Reheat, put into bottles or preserving jars, seal and sterilise. This is very good with sausages, bacon and pork.

Banana Sauce

	Imperial	Metric	American
Bananas	10	10	10
Onions	1 lb	500 g	2½ cups
Dates	1 lb	500 g	2½ cups
Golden syrup	1 lb	500 g	1½ cups
Salt	1 tbsp	1 tbsp	1 tbsp
Ground ginger	1 oz	25 g	4 tbsp
Turmeric	1 tbsp	1 tbsp	1 tbsp
Vinegar	1½ pints	750 ml	3¾ cups

Peel and mash the bananas. Mince the onions and dates together and add to the bananas. Stir in the remaining ingredients and bring to the boil. Simmer until thick and brown and then put through a sieve. Reheat, put into bottles or preserving jars, seal and sterilise.

Bramble Ketchup

	Imperial	Metric	American
Ripe blackberries	4 lb	2 kg	4 lb
Sugar	2 lb	1 kg	4 cups
Vinegar	1 pint	500 ml	2½ cups
Ground cloves	2 tsp	2 tsp	2 tsp
Ground cinnamon	2 tsp	2 tsp	2 tsp
Ground allspice	1 tsp	1 tsp	1 tsp

Put all the ingredients into a pan and bring to the boil. Simmer until thick and put through a sieve. Reheat, put into bottles or preserving jars, seal and sterilise.

Date Sauce

	Imperial	Metric	American
Dates	1 lb	500 g	1 lb
Sultanas	4 oz	100 g	¾ cup
Onions	4 oz	100 g	¾ cup
Golden syrup	4 oz	100 g	¾ cup
Salt	1 tsp	1 tsp	1 tsp
Ground ginger	1 tsp	1 tsp	1 tsp
Pepper	¼ tsp	¼ tsp	¼ tsp
Vinegar	1 pint	500 ml	2½ cups

Mince the dates, sultanas and onions. Put into a pan with all the other ingredients and bring to the boil. Simmer until thick and put through a sieve. Reheat, put into bottles or preserving jars, seal and sterilise.

Plum Sauce

	Imperial	Metric	American
Ripe plums	3 lb	1.5 kg	3 lb
Golden syrup	1½ lb	750 g	2¼ cups
Vinegar	1½ pints	750 ml	3¾ cups
Ground ginger	½ oz	15 g	1 tbsp
Salt	3 tsp	3 tsp	3 tsp
Pepper	½ tsp	½ tsp	½ tsp
Ground cloves	1 oz	25 g	1 tbsp

Put all the ingredients together in a pan and bring to the boil. Simmer for 1 hour. Put through a sieve. Reheat, put into bottles or preserving jars, seal and sterilise.

Tomato Sauce

	Imperial	Metric	American
Ripe tomatoes	6 lb	3 kg	6 lb
Onions	2 lb	1 kg	2 lb
Salt	2 oz	50 g	4 tbsp
Pepper	½ tsp	½ tsp	½ tsp
Mustard	2 tbsp	1 tbsp	2 tbsp
Golden syrup	2 lb	1 kg	1½ cups
Vinegar			

Peel the tomatoes and cut them in half. Peel and slice the onions. Put into separate bowls and sprinkle both with the salt. Leave to stand overnight. Drain and put into a pan with all the other ingredients. Bring to the boil and then simmer for 1¼ hours. Put through a sieve. Reheat, put into bottles or preserving jars, seal and sterilise.

Farmhouse Sauce

	Imperial	Metric	American
Vinegar	2 pints	1 l	5 cups
Salt	½ oz	15 g	1 tbsp
Garlic	½ oz	15 g	1 tbsp
Pepper	½ oz	15 g	1 tbsp
Ground cloves	½ oz	15 g	1 tbsp
A little black treacle			

Simmer all the ingredients for 20 minutes, and adjust sweetening to taste with the treacle. Strain and put into bottles. We like to use this with tomato juice and to season steaks.

Mustard Dressing (Non-Keeping)

1 tbsp made mustard
1 tbsp sugar
1 tbsp cornflour (cornstarch)
Pinch of pepper
1 tsp salt
1 tsp celery seed
1 pint/500 ml/2½ cups vinegar

Mix together the mustard, sugar, cornflour, pepper, salt and celery seed. Stir in the vinegar and put into a double saucepan, or a bowl over hot water. Cook until thickened and pour into a preserving jar. Keep covered in the refrigerator. This is good with beef and also with fish.

Horseradish Sauce (Non-Keeping)

2 tbsp sweetened condensed milk
1 saltsp salt
2 tbsp vinegar
2 tbsp finely grated horseradish

Stir the salt into the milk and gradually drip in the vinegar, stirring all the time. When smooth and thick, mix in the horseradish. We have this with beef and with smoked fish.

Condensed Milk Salad Dressing (Non-Keeping)

2 tbsp sweetened condensed milk
2 tbsp vinegar
½ tsp made mustard
¼ tsp pepper
½ tsp salt

Put the milk into a bowl and drip in the vinegar, stirring all the time and at the same time working in the seasonings. If you like a sharp dressing, add a little more vinegar.

Darlington Salad Cream (Non-Keeping)

1 tsp salt
1 tsp sugar
1 tsp made mustard
1 tbsp cornflour (cornstarch)
1 egg
¼ pint/125 ml/¾ cup milk
2 tbsp melted butter or margarine
2½ fl.oz/65 ml/¼ cup vinegar

Put the salt, sugar, mustard, cornflour (cornstarch), egg and milk into a pan and heat slowly, stirring well. Add the melted fat and gradually stir in the vinegar. Cook over very gentle heat until thick and creamy.

Chapter Eight

PASTES, BUTTERS AND CHEESES

Chicken Paste

	Imperial	Metric	American
Cooked chicken	1 lb	500 g	2½ cups
Cooked bacon	6 oz	175 g	1 cup
Salt and pepper			
Butter	3 oz	75 g	⅓ cup

Use all the odd bits of dark and light meat from the chicken, and pieces of a bacon joint. Mince the chicken and bacon together through a fine grinder. Mash with seasoning to taste and with softened butter. Pack into small jars and store in the refrigerator. This is very good for teatime for bread, toast or biscuits, or to use in sandwiches.

Potted Beef

	Imperial	Metric	American
Butter	8 oz	225 g	1 cup
Rump steak	1½ lb	750 g	4 cups
Salt and pepper			

Put half the butter into a casserole. Add the steak cut into small dice, and season with salt and pepper. Cover and put the casserole into a pan of hot water. Simmer for 3 hours until the beef is completely tender (no water must get into the beef). Mince the beef and mix with the liquid which has run out, and with the remaining butter. Adjust seasoning to taste. Put into small jars and cool. Cover with extra melted butter if you want to keep it longer. This is a very special teatime spread or it can be used for sandwiches.

Peanut Butter

1 lb/500 g/4 cups peanuts
½ tsp salt
1 tbsp olive oil

Put shelled peanuts into a moderate oven and heat until the pink skins will come off. Rub off the skins and mince the nuts twice to get them very fine. Add salt and oil and mix thoroughly. Put into a jar in the oven at 300°F/150°C/Gas Mark 2 for 15 minutes. Stir well to prevent burning. Cool and put into a screwtop jar. This makes a very good sandwich filling with some grated cheese.

Cheese Spread

	Imperial	Metric	American
Grated cheese	4 oz	100 g	1 cup
Butter	1 oz	25 g	2 tbsp
Salt	½ tsp	½ tsp	½ tsp
Mustard powder	½ tsp	½ tsp	½ tsp
Egg	1	1	1

Pinch of pepper

Grate the cheese finely. Cream the butter, salt, mustard, egg and pepper and work in the cheese. Put into small pots and keep in a cold place—top with melted butter if you like. This is a tasty spread on toast which can be grilled until bubbling. It can be used for sandwiches, or spread on bread instead of butter when making meat sandwiches and it enhances the filling. It uses up a hard piece of cheese perfectly.

Rum Butter

	Imperial	Metric	American
Nutmeg	½	½	½
Soft brown sugar	1 lb	500 g	2 cups
Butter	8 oz	225 g	1 cup
Rum	3 fl.oz	75 ml	⅓ cup

Grate the nutmeg into the sugar. Soften the butter and whip it into the sugar with the rum until it is soft and creamy. You can add a little more rum if you like a strong taste. Put it in a glass dish to set. We call this Brown Jam, and it is made in Cumberland for Christenings and Christmas.

Cottage Cheese

	Imperial	Metric	American
Milk	1 pint	500 ml	2½ cups
Salt			

Put the milk in a warm place by the fire and when it is completely solid, turn it carefully into a piece of muslin and hang it up to drip. Put a basin underneath to catch the whey. Leave overnight, then open the muslin and scrape the dry cheese down into the middle of the curd. Tie up and hang again overnight. Open out and put the curd on wet greaseproof paper. Salt it and mix the salt well in with a knife. Form cheese into a square block, wrap in wet greaseproof paper and keep for 5—7 days when it is an excellent cream cheese.

Goat's Cottage Cheese

I sometimes use the same method with a mixture of equal parts of goat's and cow's milk. I make small round cheeses and leave for 4 days in wet paper, then blot off moisture with white blotting paper. The cheeses need to be turned and blotted for a day or two until the dry surface forms a skin. We dry and store them on top of a jug and we keep them for about 3 weeks to ripen.

Chapter Nine

SYRUPS AND MINERALS

Home-made drinks are good for all the family and I like to make a few for the store cupboard. Such drinks are particularly healthy for children.

Dandelion Beer

	Imperial	Metric	American
Green dandelion leaves	3 oz	75 g	1 cup
Hops	2 oz	50 g	½ cup
Liquorice	½ oz	15 g	1 tbsp
Root ginger	½ oz	15 g	1 tbsp
Sugar	3 lb	1.5 kg	6 cups
Fresh yeast	½ oz	15 g	½ oz

Put the dandelion leaves, hops, liquorice and bruised ginger into a muslin bag. Put into a pan with 24 pints/14 litres/70 cups water. Boil for 30 minutes and discard the muslin bag. Stir the sugar into the hot liquid until dissolved. Leave until lukewarm and then stir in the yeast. Leave to stand overnight and put into screwtop beer or cider bottles. This will be ready for use in 2 days and is a healthy drink for children in summer time.

Elderberry Syrup

	Imperial	Metric	American
Water	2 pints	1 litre	5 cups
Elderberries	2 lb	1 kg	8 cups
Root ginger	1 piece	1 piece	1 piece
Cloves	6	6	6
Sugar			

Put the water, berries, ginger and cloves into a pan and simmer for 30 minutes. Strain and measure the liquid. Allow 8 oz/225 g/1 cup sugar to each pint/500 ml/2½ cups liquid. Boil together for 10 minutes, pour into bottles, seal and sterilise as for bottled fruit. Syrup can also be frozen in polythene containers.

Use a little in cold water for a summer drink, or with boiling water as a nightcap for a cold. Some people add 1 tablespoon gin to each pint/500 ml/2½ cups syrup.

Fruit Syrup

Use any ripe soft fruit to make syrup. You can use raspberries and redcurrants together, strawberries, black currants, blackberries, peaches, apricots or plums, which all make good syrups. Put any quantity into an earthenware casserole with ¼ pint/125 ml/½ cup water. Put on a lid and leave in the oven at

300°/150°C/Gas Mark 2 for 1 hour until the juice is running. Strain and squeeze out all the juice. Measure the liquid and allow 12 oz/350 g/1½ cups sugar to each pint/500 ml/2½ cups liquid. Boil sugar and juice together rapidly for 5 minutes, straining off scum. Bottle, seal and sterilise as for bottled fruit, or freeze in polythene containers. Use this syrup with ice cream, diluting it if it is too strong or too sweet. Use with cold water or soda water as a summer drink, or with hot water for a cold. Use as a syrup for fresh fruit salad.

Rose Syrup

	Imperial	Metric	American
Rose petals	200	200	200
Water	2 pints	1 litre	5 cups
Sugar	1 lb	450 g	2 cups

You will need about 35 fresh roses for this, and dark richly-scented red ones are best. Cut the little white point from each petal as this is bitter. Boil the water and sugar together for 2 minutes. Add rose petals and simmer gently for 30 minutes. Leave to stand overnight, then simmer again for 15 minutes. Strain into small jars and store in the refrigerator. You can use this for flavouring sponge cakes, and the leftover pulp can be used as a filling for a sandwich cake. The syrup is good with gin and hot water for a cold. Red roses are supposed to have medicinal properties. You can use 200 violets in the same amount of sugar and water for Violet Syrup.

Lemonade

	Imperial	Metric	American
Lemons	2	2	2
Orange	1	1	1
Water	1½ pints	750 ml	3¾ cups
Sugar	1½ lb	750 g	3 cups
Tartaric acid	1 oz	25 g	2 tbsp

Peel the fruit very thinly and boil the peel in the water for 5 minutes. Strain and pour over the sugar and strained fruit juice. Boil again and stir in acid. Bottle and store in the refrigerator. Dilute to taste. This is good in hot weather, but can be used with boiling water as a nightcap for a cold.

Fruit Vinegar

Use raspberries, loganberries, blackberries or blackcurrants. Cover the fruit with white vinegar and mash it each day for 4 or 5 days, stirring well. Strain and measure the juice and allow 1 lb/500 g/2 cups sugar to each pint/500 ml/2½ cups juice. Boil for 10 minutes and put into bottles. Dilute with cold water or soda for a summer drink, or add boiling water for a nightcap. Children always used to be given raspberry vinegar for their colds. In Yorkshire, they use fruit vinegar as a sauce for plain suet and rice puddings, and it is good and tasty.

Chapter Ten

FARMHOUSE SPECIALS

These days, not many of us have our own sheep and pigs to kill and use. We used to cure our own sheepskins, make soup from sheep's head, and make up the meat in various ways. We used to render down the fat and whip it up with rosewater to make handcream, and the leftover bits of fat and skin we used to render down and use to waterproof boots and keep the leather soft. We even used to make soap from surplus fat. Every bit of the pig used to be taken care of except the squeak. Pigs used to be killed just before Christmas and the pieces of pork often made presents for the farm men. We made our own lard, black and white puddings, and bacon. These are some of our specialities from the good old days.

Pork Sausages

	Imperial	Metric	American
Pork	1 lb	500 g	2½ cups
Breadcrumbs	4 oz	100 g	1⅓ cups

Salt and pepper
Pinch of sage or marjoram

Use pork which is half fat and half lean. Put through the mincer. Soak the breadcrumbs in cold water and squeeze them almost dry. Mix with the meat and season well. Either fill sausage skins with a hand-filler or with an attachment on an electric mincer, or just form the mixture into sausage shapes. Keep in the refrigerator or freeze them for later use.

Pork Pie

	Imperial	Metric	American
Plain flour	1 lb	500 g	4 cups
Lard	5 oz	125 g	¾ cup
Salt	½ tsp	½ tsp	½ tsp
Boiling water			
Pork	1 lb	500 g	2½ cups
Salt and pepper			

Rub the lard into the flour, add salt and use a little boiling water to mix. Knead well and leave on one side for an hour, but do not let it get cold. Mould a pie shape over the end of a jam jar, getting the walls of an even thickness. Cut the pork into very small pieces, or mince it. Season well and put into the pastry case. Add a spoonful of water. Put on a pastry lid and pinch the edges together. Make a hole in the centre and decorate with leaves of pastry. Brush all over with a little egg beaten with a pinch of salt. Bake at 425°F/220°C/Gas Mark 7 for 20 minutes, then at 350°F/180°C/Gas Mark 4 for 1 hour. Cover the pastry if it is getting too brown. Meanwhile, simmer any pork bones or trimmings in a little water to make a rich stock. Leave until it has almost turned to jelly. Pour a little into the hole in the lid when the pie comes out of the oven, and then when the pie is cold.

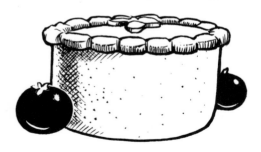

Beef Roll

	Imperial	Metric	American
Lean beef	1¼ lb	625 g	3½ cups
Bacon	1 lb	500 g	2½ cups
Breadcrumbs	8 oz	225 g	3 cups
Salt and pepper			
Egg	1	1	1
Hard-boiled eggs	2	2	2

Mince together the beef, bacon and breadcrumbs. Season well and bind with the beaten egg. Flatten out to a square and put the hard-boiled eggs in the middle. Roll up into a neat cylinder. Wrap in greased paper and then steam for 2 hours. Remove paper and cool, and if liked dust with browned breadcrumbs. This is good to 'cut and come again' in summer or winter.

Pressed Beef

3 lb/1.5 kg beef brisket
Salt and pepper
1 tbsp gelatine

Roll the brisket and tie it into shape. Put in a pan, cover with water and season well. Bring to the boil, skim, and then simmer gently for 4 hours until tender. Cool slightly and then put into a basin or large mould. Put a plate on top and a weight to press it. Strain the liquid and measure out ¾ pint/375 ml/1¼ cups liquid. Stir the gelatine into a little of the liquid and dissolve over heat until the gelatine is syrupy. Add to the measured liquid and pour over the meat. Leave until set and jellied. I do a tongue this way too.

Meat Glaze

	Imperial	Metric	American
Stock	¼ pint	125 ml	½ cup
Beef cube	1	1	1
Gelatine	¼ oz	8 g	½ tbsp

Dissolve the beef cube in the stock and stir in the gelatine. Heat gently and keep stirring until liquid is smooth and clear. Season to taste with salt and pepper. Brush over any cold meat and allow to set, then brush over again, using two or three 'coats'. The glaze should be cool when used and is good for any cooked meat.

We like making our own sweets too, and toffee is particularly popular. We test it after boiling by dropping a little into a cup of cold water. If it sets at once and breaks with a 'crack' it is ready to pour into the tin.

Hinderwell Toffee

	Imperial	Metric	American
Butter	5 oz	125 g	½ cup
Sugar	5 oz	125 g	½ cup
Golden syrup	2 oz	50 g	¼ cup
Single cream	2 tbsp	2 tbsp	2 tbsp

Beat together the butter and sugar as if making a cake and work in the syrup and cream. Stir well and then boil for 20 minutes. Pour into a buttered tin, cool, and then cut into squares and wrap in paper.

Leadgate Toffee

	Imperial	Metric	American
Butter	4 oz	100 g	½ cup
Sugar	6 oz	175 g	¾ cup
Vinegar	3 tbsp	3 tbsp	3 tbsp
Golden syrup	3 tbsp	3 tbsp	3 tbsp
Water	2 tbsp	2 tbsp	2 tbsp
Lemon essence			

Put all the ingredients into a pan and stir over low heat until the sugar has dissolved. Boil fast to a set and pour into a greased tin. Break in pieces when cold.

Peggy's Toffee

	Imperial	Metric	American
Butter	6 oz	175 g	¾ cup
Sugar	1 lb	500 g	2 cups
Vinegar	4 tbsp	4 tbsp	4 tbsp

Melt the butter and stir in the sugar. Dissolve over low heat, then add vinegar and stir until it boils. Boil hard for 6 minutes and then pour into a greased tin. Break in pieces when cold. Never stir after it boils. These toffees are good for a cold and with a tin of Peggy's Toffee on the shelf, one is the best granny or auntie in the whole world.

Stanhope Toffee

	Imperial	Metric	American
Sugar	1 lb	500 g	2 cups
Butter	4 oz	100 g	½ cup
Single cream	1 tbsp	1 tbsp	1 tbsp
Condensed milk	2 tbsp	2 tbsp	2 tbsp
Golden syrup	2 tbsp	2 tbsp	2 tbsp
Vinegar	2 tbsp	2 tbsp	2 tbsp
Almonds	2 oz	50 g	½ cup

Blanch and skin the almonds and divide them in half. Put all the other ingredients into a pan and stir until the sugar has dissolved. Bring to the boil and do not stir again. After 5 minutes, test for setting, and when it is ready, pour into a greased tin. Arrange the almonds on top and leave until cold before breaking in pieces.

Chapter Eleven

USEFUL HOUSEHOLD RECIPES

Many herbs can be grown in the garden and they are so useful.

Mint is cut in our garden in August or September and dried in the kitchen inside a paper bag to keep the dust off. I rub off the dry crackly leaves just before Christmas and keep them in a tightly lidded jar. You can use these dried leaves for mint tea which is very good for colic and wind in the stomach.

Sage is done in the same way as mint, and is very useful for sage and onion stuffing with a winter joint of pork, or a fat duck or goose.

Marjoram is my favourite herb for puddings, stuffings and sausages, and I dry it the same way when the flowers have just finished.

Lavender is good burned on a shovel to drive out offensive smells, and it leaves a lovely fragrance.

Marigolds used to be used a lot. You just dry the flowers and add them to soup, salads or cream cheese. You don't need much, but they are very tasty.

Cough Cure

	Imperial	Metric	American
Cod liver oil	2 fl.oz	50 ml	¼ cup
Honey	2 oz	50 g	½ cup
Juice of lemons	4	4	4

Shake all the ingredients together and take them often. A good dose is 2 teaspoons each time.

Cough Cure for an Old Person

2 tbsp brown sugar
Juice of 2 lemons
1 tbsp olive oil
1 pint/500 ml/2½ cups boiling water
Add the water to the other ingredients and stir well until dissolved. Put into a bottle, and give 1 tablespoon mixture each time. It is very soothing.

Mincemeat

	Imperial	Metric	American
Raisins	1 lb	500 g	3 cups
Currants	8 oz	225 g	1½ cups
Shredded suet	1 lb	500 g	4 cups
Apples	3 lb	1.5 kg	3 lb
Sugar	1½ lb	750 g	3 cups
Candied peel	4 oz	100 g	1 cup
Ground nutmeg	1 tsp	1 tsp	1 tsp
Ground mixed spice	1 tsp	1 tsp	1 tsp
Grated rind of lemon	1	1	1

Chop the raisins. Peel, core and chop the apples. Mix all the ingredients together and put into screwtop preserving jars. Keep in a cool place. I usually make this a couple of weeks before Christmas. Sometimes I add a few chopped almonds, and you can put in some brandy, sherry or rum.

Breadcrumbs

We make breadcrumbs in different ways and they are so useful. Try putting clean stale bread crusts through the mincer and then dry them for a few minutes in the oven. Use in a plum pudding or suet pudding to make them lighter, or keep them on hand for fruit charlottes. You can also make crumbs by grating bread on a grater and drying the crumbs in the oven. I find them very useful for coating food which is to be fried.

Seaham Harbour Hand Cream

2 tbsp glycerine
4 tbsp methylated spirits
4 tbsp milk
1 egg white

Mix all the ingredients together and bottle. Use after washing your hands and on going to bed, and rub the cream well in. This helps to keep hands nice after washing-up.

Pot Pourri

Gather flowers on a dry calm day, and use such perfumed flowers and leaves as rose petals, lavender, thyme, verbena and stock. Spread on paper or a rack in a dry place and turn the petals often so they dry. Put into a jar and sprinkle clean dry cooking salt between each layer. Stand in a dry place for 2 weeks. Add 1 oz/25 g/1 tablespoon cloves, 1 oz/25 g/cinnamon stick, 1 oz/25 g/1 tablespoon allspice and a grated nutmeg. Cover with a close-fitting lid. Sprinkle with a little orange-flower water or eau-de-cologne if liked. This will keep fragrant for years, but should only be left open for 30 minutes each day.

Chapter Twelve

FREEZING

Freezing is the newest way of preserving food, and it is a very useful way of keeping fruit, vegetables and meat in particular, but I also like to keep some of my cooked dishes and cakes too ready for unexpected visitors.

Vegetables

We always freeze small quantities of vegetables at a time, fresh from the garden. If you save them up until a lot are ready, it means the work is very tiring, and also some of the vegetables are too old to freeze really well. I like to pick early in the day and prepare the vegetables when I am getting some ready for our midday meal.

I use a big saucepan for preparing the vegetables and a wire basket (I use my chip basket). The saucepan holds about 8 pints/5 litres/20 cups water and I bring it to the boil, then put in 1 lb/500 g/3 cups prepared vegetables. Then the lid goes on and the water has to come back to the boil quickly. As soon as it boils, I start timing. Most vegetables only need 1—2 minutes cooking (or blanching) like this. Then they go straight into ice-cold water, because running tap water just isn't cold enough. When they are chilled, I dry them on kitchen paper and pack straight into polythene bags or boxes for freezing. You can do most vegetables like that, but I think peas and beans are the nicest. Small young carrots can be good, and of course sprouts, but I don't bother much with greenstuff which will stand in the garden, and the same goes for roots too. Salads don't freeze well, because there is so much water in them, but I always prepare a few bags of tomatoes because they are so useful for cooking in the winter. They don't need any special treatment, and I just wipe them and pack into bags for freezing.

Fruit

Fruit is really lovely in the freezer and it is marvellous to have our own raspberries at Christmas. I usually just put berries or currants into bags and freeze them without sugar as they are so much more useful afterwards. If I have a lot of fruit and not much space, I cook it first and then make it into sweet purée for freezing. You can freeze fruit in dry sugar too, or in syrup, but that takes longer and I don't think there is much point as it can be cooked and sweetened later. Apples need sugar or syrup though, or they will discolour, and the same goes for peaches and apricots.

Meat, Poultry and Game

We often have our own meat and poultry to freeze, and sometimes game. I think it is important to freeze it in just the way I am going to use it, or it takes ages to prepare afterwards. That means boning and rolling meat, or cutting it into useful pieces, and of course poultry and game must be plucked or skinned, and cleaned before freezing. Pack meat or poultry into polythene and take out all the air. It is important to freeze these things quickly for the best results. I like to thaw them thoroughly before cooking for really tasty juicy meat, and it is very important indeed to thaw out poultry or the centre may not be thoroughly cooked which can be dangerous.

Cooked Dishes

When I feel like cooking a lot, I make a few extra things for the freezer. Mostly I freeze stews and soups which I usually put into foil containers which can be used for reheating. Pies and puddings freeze well too, and don't take long to reheat. Quite often, I take small cooked pies or pasties out of the freezer and put them into the men's lunchboxes, and they are thawed and ready by the middle of the day. I like to keep a few cakes in too – scones are very useful, and one or two sponges and butter-iced cakes, while a few loaves of bread are a good standby if the weather is bad. They only need wrapping in polythene and freezing quickly.

There really aren't many rules about freezing. I find it is important to be very clean and to keep everything cool in the kitchen. All air has to come out of packages, and it is important to freeze food quickly for good results. I cook thin pieces of meat and fish while still frozen, and of course vegetables don't need thawing either. Everything else is best thawed slowly in the refrigerator.

INDEX

A
Annfield Plain Blackcurrant
    Jam **11**
Annfield Plain Rhubarb Jam **11**
Annfield Plain Winter Jam **12**
Apple Chutney **53**
Apple and Blackberry Jam **14**
Apple and Damson Jelly **28**
Apple Ginger Jam **13**
Apple Marmalade **34**
Apple and Grapefruit Marmalade **35**
Apple (Newton) Chutney **61**
Apple and Red Tomato Chutney **54**
Apple Sauce **67**
Apricot (Crofton) Jam **17**
Apricot (Fresh) Jam **12**

B
Banana Chutney **55**
Banana Sauce **68**
Beef (Potted) **74**
Beef (Pressed) **83**
Beef Roll **83**
Bishopton Chutney **54**
Blackberry Jam **13**
Blackberry and Apple Jam **14**
Blackcurrant Jam **15**
Blackcurrant (Annfield Plain)
    Jam **11**
Blackcurrant and Rhubarb Jam **14**
Blackcurrant Jelly **26**
Bramble Curd **15**
Bramble Jelly **26**
Bramble Ketchup **68**
Breadcrumbs **89**

C
Cabbage Pickle **44**
Cabbage (Red) Pickle **51**
Cheese Spread **75**
Cherries (Pickled) **45**
Cherry Plum Jam **16**
Chicken Paste **73**
Chutneys:
    Apple **53**
    Apple (Newton) **61**
    Apple and Red Tomato **54**
    Banana **55**
    Bishopton **54**
    Date (No Cook) **56**
    Gooseberry **56**

Green Plum **57**
Green Tomato **58**
Lanchester **58**
Mixed Autumn **60**
Mrs Latchem's **59**
Marrow **66**
Newton Apple **61**
No Cook Date **56**
Onion and Tomato **64**
Orange **60**
Peggy's Pear **62**
Plum (Green) **56**
Red Tomato **65**
Red Tomato and Apple **54**
Rhubarb **64**
Stanhope Rhubarb **62**
Thornton-Le-Dale **63**
Tomato (Green) **58**
Tomato (Red) **65**
Tomato and Onion **64**
Condensed Milk Salad Dressing **72**
Cottage Cheese **76**
Cottage Cheese (Goat's) **76**
Cottage Marmalade **34**
Cough Cure **87**
Cough Cure for an Old Person **88**
Country Jam **16**
Crabapple Jelly **27**
Crofton Apricot Jam **17**
Curd, Bramble **15**
Curd, Lemon **18**

D
Damson and Apple Jelly **28**
Damsons (Pickled) **46**
Dandelion Beer **77**
Darlington Salad Cream **72**
Date Jam **17**
Date (No Cook) Chutney **56**
Date and Rhubarb Jam **21**
Date Sauce **69**
Dressings:
    Condensed Milk Salad **72**
    Mustard **71**
    Darlington Salad Cream **72**

E
Elderberry (Mrs Shenton's) Jelly **29**
Elderberry Syrup **78**

F

Farmhouse Sauce **70**
Fig and Rhubarb Jam **22**
Fig Pickle **45**
French Beans (Pickled) **46**
Fruit (Freezing) **92**
Fruit Syrup **78**
Fruit Vinegar **80**

G

Ginger and Apple Jam **13**
Ginger and Rhubarb Jam **23**
Goat's Cottage Cheese **76**
Gooseberry Chutney **56**
Grapefruit and Apple
    Marmalade **35**
Green Gooseberry Jam **18**
Green Gooseberry Mint Jelly **28**
Green Plum Chutney **57**
Green Tomato Chutney **58**
Green Tomato Marmalade **39**
Green Walnuts Pickle **48**

H

Hand Cream (Seaham Harbour) **89**
Hinderwell Toffee **84**
Horseradish Sauce **71**

J

Jams:
    Annfield Plain Blackcurrant **11**
    Annfield Plain Rhubarb **11**
    Annfield Plain Winter **12**
    Apple and Blackberry **14**
    Apple Ginger **13**
    Apricot (Crofton) **17**
    Apricot (Fresh) **12**
    Blackberry **13**
    Blackberry and Apple **14**
    Blackcurrant **15**
    Blackcurrant and Rhubarb **14**
    Bramble Curd **15**
    Cherry Plum **16**
    Country Jam **16**
    Crofton Apricot **17**
    Date **17**
    Date and Rhubarb **21**
    Fig and Rhubarb **22**
    Ginger and Rhubarb **23**
    Green Gooseberry **18**
    Lemon Curd **18**
    Marrow **19**
    Orchard (1) **20**
    Orchard (2) **20**
    Raspberry **21**

    Raspberry and Stawberry **23**
    Rhubarb (Annfield) **11**
    Rhubarb and Date Jam **21**
    Rhubarb and Fig Jam **22**
    Rhubarb and Ginger Jam **23**
    Strawberry and Raspberry **23**
    Strawberry and Redcurrant **24**
    Strawberry and Rhubarb **24**
Jellies:
    Apple and Damson **28**
    Blackcurrant **26**
    Bramble **26**
    Crabapple **27**
    Damson and Apple **28**
    Elderberry (Mrs Shenton's) **29**
    Green Gooseberry Mint Jelly **28**
    Lemon **31**
    Mint **30**
    Mint, Green Gooseberry **28**
    Mrs Shenton's Elderberry **29**
    Orange **31**
    Raspberry and Redcurrant **32**
    Redcurrant **31**
    Redcurrant and Raspberry **32**
    Rowanberry **32**

K

Ketchup, Bramble **68**

L

Lanchester Chutney **58**
Leeks (Pickled) **47**
Leadgate Toffee **85**
Lemonade **80**
Lemon Curd **18**
Lemon Jelly **31**

M

Marmalades:
    Apple **34**
    Apple and Grapefruit **35**
    Cottage **34**
    Grapefruit and Apple **35**
    Green Tomato **39**
    Orange **38**
    Pear **36**
    Rhubarb **39**
    Sadberge **37**
    Tomato (Green) **39**
    Trinity **40**
Marrow Chutney **66**
Marrow Jam **19**
Meat Glaze **84**
Meat, Poultry and Game
    (Freezing) **92**
Mincemeat **80**

Mint Jelly **30**
Mint, Green Gooseberry Jelly **28**
Mixed Autumn Chutney **60**
Mixed Pickle **50**
Mustard Dressing **71**
Mustard Pickle **49**
Mrs Latchem's Chutney **59**
Mrs Shenton's Elderberry Jelly **29**

N
Nasturtiums (Pickled) **48**
Newton Apple Chutney **61**
No-Cook Date Chutney **56**

O
Onions or Shallots (Pickled) **52**
Onion and Tomato Chutney **64**
Orange Chutney **60**
Orange Jelly **31**
Orange Marmalade **38**
Orchard Jam (1) **20**
Orchard Jam (2) **20**

P
Peanut Butter **74**
Pear (Peggy's) Chutney **62**
Pear Marmalade **36**
Peggy's Pear Chutney **62**
Peggy's Toffee **85**
Pickles:
    Cabbage **44**
    Cherries **45**
    Damsons **46**
    Fig **45**
    French Beans **46**
    Green Walnuts **48**
    Leeks **47**
    Mixed **50**
    Mustard **49**
    Nasturtiums **48**
    Prune **51**
    Red Cabbage **51**
    Onions or Shallots **52**
Plum (Green) Chutney **56**
Plum Sauce **69**
Pork Pie **82**
Pork Sausages **81**
Pot Pourri **90**
Potted Beef **74**
Poultry and Game (Freezing) **92**
Pressed Beef **83**
Prune Pickle **51**

R
Raspberry Jam **21**
Raspberry and Redcurrant Jelly **32**

Raspberry and Strawberry Jam **23**
Red Cabbage Pickle **51**
Redcurrant Jelly **31**
Redcurrant and Raspberry Jelly **32**
Redcurrant and Strawberry Jam **24**
Red Tomato Chutney **65**
Rhubarb (Annfield Plain) Jam **11**
Rhubarb Chutney **64**
Rhubarb (Stanhope) Chutney **62**
Rhubarb and Date Jam **21**
Rhubarb and Fig Jam **22**
Rhubarb and Ginger Jam **23**
Rhubarb Marmalade **39**
Rhubarb and Strawberry Jam **24**
Rose Syrup **79**
Rowanberry Jelly **32**
Rum Butter **75**

S
Sadberge Marmalade **37**
Sauces:
    Apple **67**
    Banana **68**
    Date **69**
    Farmhouse **70**
    Horseradish **71**
    Plum **69**
    Tomato **70**
Seaham Harbour Hand Cream **89**
Shallots or Onions (Pickled) **52**
Stanhope Rhubarb Chutney **62**
Stanhope Toffee **86**
Strawberry and Raspberry Jam **23**
Strawberry and Redcurrant
    Jam **24**
Strawberry and Rhubarb Jam **24**

T
Thornton-Le-Dale Chutney **63**
Toffee (Hinderwell) **84**
    Leadgate **85**
    Peggy's **85**
    Stanhope **86**
Tomato (Green) Chutney **58**
Tomato (Green) Marmalade **39**
Tomato (Red) Chutney **65**
Tomato (Red) and Apple Chutney **54**
Tomato and Onion Chutney **64**
Tomato Sauce **70**
Trinity Marmalade **40**

V
Vegetables (Freezing) **91**

W
Walnuts (Green) Pickle **48**